BRAZIL

BY ANDREA PELLESCHI

Essential Library

An Imprint of Abdo Publishing
abdobooks.com

ABDOBOOKS.COM

Published by Abdo Publishing, a division of ABDO, PO Box 398166, Minneapolis, Minnesota 55439. Copyright © 2023 by Abdo Consulting Group, Inc. International copyrights reserved in all countries. No part of this book may be reproduced in any form without written permission from the publisher. Essential Library™ is a trademark and logo of Abdo Publishing.

Printed in the United States of America, North Mankato, Minnesota.
102022
012023

Cover Photos: Shutterstock Images (Rio de Janeiro, pattern)
Interior Photos: Shutterstock Images, 4–5, 10, 23, 28, 33, 34, 38, 65, 69, 94; Aleksandar Todorovic/Shutterstock Images, 7, 9; Eric Isselee/Shutterstock Images, 13; Donatas Dabravolskas/Shutterstock Images, 14–15; Bernard Barroso/Shutterstock Images, 16–17; Nido Huebl/Shutterstock Images, 20; Peter Hermes Furian/Shutterstock Images, 21 (Brazil); Web Tools/Shutterstock Images, 21 (globe); Uwe Bergwitz/Shutterstock Images, 24–25; Milan Zygmunt/Shutterstock Images, 26–27; Martin Pelanek/Shutterstock Images, 30; Patrick K. Campbell/Shutterstock Images, 35; Cacio Murilo/Shutterstock Images, 36–37; Ricardo Ribas/SOPA Images/Light Rocket/Getty Images, 40–41; Pictures From History/Universal Images Group/Getty Images, 43; Sepia Times/Universal Images Group/Getty Images, 45; PHAS/Universal Images Group/Getty Images, 47; UtCon Collection/Alamy, 48; Photo 12/Universal Images Group/Getty Images, 49, 95; AP Images, 52; David Goldman/AP Images, 55; Ricardo Cohen/Shutterstock Images, 56–57; Cris Faga/NurPhoto/Getty Images, 59; Alf Ribeiro/Shutterstock Images, 61, 86; The History Collection/Alamy, 63; Andre Coria/Shutterstock Images, 64; Buda Mendes/Getty Images News/Getty Images, 67; Diego Grandi/Shutterstock Images, 70–71, 74; BW Press/Shutterstock Images, 72; Cintia Erdens Paiva/Alamy, 78; Alena Zharava/Shutterstock Images, 80–81; Albert Russ/Shutterstock Images, 82; Antonio Scorza/Shutterstock Images, 83; Kedson Carvalho/Shutterstock Images, 84; R. Augustus/Shutterstock Images, 88; Marcos Casiano/Shutterstock Images, 90–91; Pascal Rondeau/Getty Images Sport/Getty Images, 93; Clive Mason/Getty Images Sport/Getty Images, 96; Andre Coelho/Getty Images News/Getty Images, 99; H. Studio/Shutterstock Images, 101

Editor: Layna Darling
Series Designer: Maggie Villaume

Library of Congress Control Number: 2022940132

PUBLISHER'S CATALOGING-IN-PUBLICATION DATA

Names: Pelleschi, Andrea, author.
Title: Brazil / by Andrea Pelleschi
Description: Minneapolis, Minnesota: Abdo Publishing, 2023 | Series: Essential Library of Countries | Includes online resources and index.
Identifiers: ISBN 9781532199370 (lib. bdg.) | ISBN 9781098274573 (ebook)
Subjects: LCSH: Brazil--Juvenile literature. | South America--Juvenile literature. | Brazil--History--Juvenile literature. | Geography--Juvenile literature.
Classification: DDC 981--dc23

CONTENTS

A TOUR OF BRAZIL

Olivia da Silva can't wait to start her vacation in Brazil. Her great-grandparents emigrated from Brazil to the United States, so she is eager to see where they came from. Her father is especially interested in visiting the country of his ancestors. Olivia's mom wants to experience the culture. And Olivia is most looking forward to seeing the Amazon Rain Forest. She wants to be a veterinarian one day and hopes to catch a glimpse of the animals that call Brazil home, such as monkeys, sloths, and anacondas.

The Amazon Rain Forest is one of the world's greatest natural wonders, and it is central to Brazil's identity.

RIO DE JANEIRO: THE JOURNEY BEGINS

Olivia and her parents fly into Rio de Janeiro, Brazil's second-largest city. Between two and six million Indigenous people inhabited the region near the Amazon before European settlers arrived.[1] In 1502, the Portuguese explorer Gonçalo Coelho was the first European to sail into what would later be called Guanabara Bay, where Rio was eventually built. Over the next several hundred years, the Portuguese colonized the area, and Rio became the capital of Brazil in 1822. It remained the capital until 1960, when the seat of the government was moved to Brasília. Today, Rio is a thriving commercial and financial center, as well as a major tourist destination.

Considered one of the most beautiful cities in the world, Rio de Janeiro is nestled between Guanabara Bay and the Atlantic Ocean. It sits on a narrow strip of land bounded by lush mountains and golden beaches. Rio's culture, landscapes, and architecture made it the first urban area to be included on the World Heritage List in 2012. The United Nations Educational, Scientific, and Cultural Organization (UNESCO) created this list to preserve natural and cultural heritage sites around the world.

At 8,300 acres (3,360 ha), Tijuca National Park is the largest urban rain forest in the world.[2]

After the da Silvas check in to their hotel, they take a taxi to Tijuca National Park, where visitors behold the rain forest's waterfalls, caves, and mountains. The park has many trails, and Olivia loves the one her family decides to hike. After that, the family rides a train to the top

The city of Rio de Janeiro features extraordinary scenic views.

of Mount Corcovado. This mountain, whose name means "hunchback," is 2,310 feet (704 m) high and provides spectacular views of Rio.[3] Olivia can see the blue waters of Guanabara Bay, the geometric skyscrapers of downtown Rio, and the pointed hulk of Sugar Loaf mountain.

But the real sight is the iconic Christ the Redeemer statue, which sits atop Mount Corcovado. This enormous sculpture of Jesus stands guard over Rio with outstretched arms, a bowed head, and loose robes. It can be seen from almost all spots around Rio, especially when the statue is lit up at night.

For dinner, Olivia and her parents head back down the mountain and take a tram to the hillside neighborhood of Santa Teresa. Once home to rich coffee barons, many of the old mansions still stand on the cobbled streets. Some mansions are in disrepair, but others have been restored as studios for the writers, musicians, and artists who live there. Since Santa Teresa has many traditional restaurants, Olivia's dad can enjoy some of the dishes his grandmother used to make. The whole family feasts on feijoada, a rich stew of beans, beef, and pork.

The rest of the week, the da Silvas sightsee around Rio. Olivia loves visiting the famous Ipanema and Copacabana beaches, and her mom enjoys soaking up the culture in Rio's historic center on the mouth of Guanabara Bay. Until the capital moved to Brasília, this area was the political center of the country. Today, it is a bustling commercial district with baroque churches, wide plazas, and historic buildings tucked next to high-rises. Baroque is a style of European

architecture from the 1700s and 1800s that features many decorations and ornate details. The da Silvas tour the Imperial Palace, where many significant events in Brazilian history took place. Here, the Golden Law was enacted in 1888. This momentous law abolished slavery in Brazil.

NEXT ON THE LIST: SALVADOR

From Rio, Olivia and her parents travel up the coast to the city of Salvador. Founded in 1549, Salvador was the first capital of the Portuguese colony of Brazil. It remained so until 1763, when the colonial capital was moved to Rio de Janeiro. Salvador struggled from the late 1700s through the mid-1900s, which is when the city's population and economy rapidly grew. Today, Salvador is a thriving city and has one of the major ports in Brazil.

Olivia's mom wants to see the historic center of Salvador, which was designated a UNESCO World Heritage site in 1985. The area has several picturesque neighborhoods, including the notable Pelourinho. The da Silvas wander the cobblestone streets amid a riot of yellow, salmon, green, and blue buildings with white trim and wrought-iron balconies. They admire the colonial mansions and ornate baroque churches with golden domes. At the central triangle-shaped square called Largo do Pelourinho, they talk about how Pelourinho was one of several spots in Salvador where enslaved people were punished. *Pelourinho* means "pillory," a wooden frame that can be used as a whipping post. Salvador hosted the first market of enslaved people in the Western Hemisphere. Echoes of this history are evident throughout the town center.

As the da Silvas continue their walk, they're overwhelmed by the many beautiful churches and museums to visit. Olivia picks the Church of the Third Order of Our Lady of the Rosary of the Black People as their first tour. She likes how the light-blue church with ornate gold trim and tiered domes stands out from the smaller buildings beside it. Its history as a church for Black people who could not worship anywhere else captures her attention.

HISTORIC CHURCH

The Church of the Third Order of Our Lady of the Rosary of the Black People was under construction for decades. In 1704, the king of Portugal gave the land for the church to the Brotherhood of Black Men. It was meant to be a church for Black people, both freed and enslaved, who were banned from other churches. But because many of the workers were enslaved people and could work only in their spare time, construction went slowly. It took almost 100 years for the church to be completed. Statues of Black saints adorn the inside, and a cemetery for enslaved people is behind the church.

LAST STOP: THE AMAZON RAIN FOREST

After several more days in Salvador, Olivia and her parents fly into Santarém, a town at the mouth of the Tapajós River. The river is a tributary of the mighty Amazon. Santarém is about halfway between the larger cities of Belém and Manaus, both on the Amazon. People have lived in the Santarém region for thousands of years. The Jesuits built a mission there in 1661, and in 1758, the city of Santarém was born.

After checking in to their hotel, the da Silvas walk around the waterfront and take in the Meeting of the Waters. This is where the blue water of the Tapajós flows alongside the yellow-brown of the Amazon. This goes on for several miles, like two parallel ribbons of color, before the waters finally mix together.

After lunch on the riverfront, Olivia soon fulfills her wish to see the rain forest up close. A rain forest is a tropical woodland with high temperatures, humidity, and rainfall, and where the tallest trees form a canopy high in the forest. Because the Amazon Rain Forest is so vast, the da Silvas have many options for how to experience it. They choose the Maicá Lake floodplains, known for their animal sightings. This is a good choice because it is often hard to spot animals in the immensity of the rain forest.

The Amazon Rain Forest spans South America from the Andes to the Atlantic Ocean. It is not only the largest tropical rain forest in the world, but it also contains the most varied life-forms. Several million species of insects, birds, and other animals and plants live in the forest, with more species still being discovered. Olivia and her parents pile into canoes with a tour guide and paddle between trees and over the calm waters of the floodplains. Olivia is thrilled to spot toucans, pink dolphins, howler monkeys, and a sloth. The day ends with a beautiful sunset on the water.

The next day, the da Silvas visit the Tapajós National Forest, a pristine area that the Brazilian government has protected from logging and development. A guide leads Olivia and her parents on a trail into the dense forest with a high canopy that blocks most of the sun. Along the walk, they see rubber plants, Brazil nut trees, and giant samaúma trees, the largest and tallest in the forest. They also spot king vultures, squirrel monkeys, capuchin monkeys, and a golden, tower-shaped termite nest sticking up from the forest floor.

After their tour, the da Silvas go back to Santarém for *tacacá*, a local food. Tacacá is a soup made of wild manioc—also called cassava or yuca—which is a root vegetable similar to a potato. The soup also has yellow peppers, dried shrimp, and an herb called *jambu*. While Olivia and her family enjoy the delicious soup, they share memories of their favorite parts of the trip. Their long flight home will depart the following day, and they all agree this tasty meal is the perfect end to an exciting vacation.

CAPUCHIN MONKEYS

Capuchin monkeys are some of the most intelligent monkeys in Central and South America. They are named after Capuchin monks because of the markings on their bodies that resemble monks' cowls. These monkeys can be light tan, dark brown, or black, and they have opposable thumbs, round heads, and prehensile tails. These are tails that can grab and hold objects, such as branches and vines. The monkeys live in troops and like to spend time in the treetops.

Brazil's natural beauty makes it a beloved home for Brazilians and a popular destination for international tourists.

BRAZIL: DISCOVERING THE FUTURE

What Olivia and her parents experienced in Brazil is just a small part of what the country has to offer. It is a land of ocean harbors, immense forests, and large cities, such as São Paulo, Rio de Janeiro, and the capital, Brasília. It is home to many people of European, African, and Indigenous ancestry.

Brazil's future remains full of opportunity. It is a world leader in mining, agriculture, and manufacturing. The country is also a leading producer of coffee and sugar. But it faces many challenges, such as deforestation in the Amazon, social inequalities, and financial crises.

Brazil holds a unique place in South America. It did not split into smaller countries the way Spanish and English colonies on the continent did after they became independent. Instead, it remained one nation after breaking free from Portugal. This long-lasting, shared identity helps unite Brazilians as they work toward a better future.

CHAPTER TWO

GEOGRAPHY

At 3.3 million square miles (8.5 million sq km), Brazil is the largest country in South America.[1] Compared with the rest of the world, it is ranked fifth in land area. Only Russia, Canada, China, and the United States are larger. Most of Brazil lies south of the equator. The eastern side of the country borders the Atlantic Ocean for 4,600 miles (7,400 km), and the rest of Brazil borders every country in South America except Chile and Ecuador.[2]

Brazil contains a wide variety of landscapes, including savannas, plateaus, low mountains, and wetlands. Its climate ranges from tropical to semi-arid. Several major river systems flow through the country's borders. Brazil has five geographic regions with

Steep canyons lush with plant life can be found in southern Brazil.

distinct physical features: the Amazon Lowlands, the Guiana Highlands, the Pantanal, the Brazilian Highlands, and the Coastal Lowlands.

The Amazon Lowlands make up part of the immense Amazon River basin, the largest river basin in the world. A river basin is the land where a river and its tributaries drain. The Amazon River basin has an area of 2.7 million square miles (7 million sq km).[3] The river and its many tributaries lay mostly within Brazil, but the river also flows through Peru, Colombia, Bolivia, Venezuela, and Ecuador. The Amazon Lowlands consist of floodplains, areas that flood annually and enrich the soil, and higher landforms called *terra firme*. Gentle hills, lakes, and wetlands are part of the terrain.

The Guiana Highlands stretch through northern Brazil, southern Venezuela, southeastern Colombia, and most of South America's Guianas region. The highlands have rolling hills at less than 1,000 feet (300 m) above sea level, low mountains in the 2,000- to 3,000-foot (600 to 900 m) range, and higher plateaus topped with sandstone. The highest point in Brazil is Neblina Peak, at the Venezuelan border, with an elevation of 9,888 feet (3,014 m).[4] The region experiences plenty of rainfall, and the lush terrain is filled with forests, rivers, and waterfalls.

The Pantanal lies in south-central Brazil, as well as northeastern Paraguay and eastern Bolivia. The Paraguay River and several of its tributaries flow through the region. The Pantanal is the largest freshwater wetland in the world. From November to March, the rivers flood, creating an assortment of swamps, marshes, and lakes. From April to September, the water recedes from all but the lowest areas, leaving sediments that enrich the soil.

The Brazilian Highlands take up more than half the land in the country, and they are known for their abundant minerals. Located in central and southeastern Brazil, they consist of rolling hills, rocky outcroppings, deep ravines, steep cliffs, and flat-topped areas called plateaus. The terrain is similar to the Guiana Highlands in the north. The Brazilian Highlands contain several mountain ranges, including the Serra Grande and Araripe Upland in the east and the Diamantina Upland in the southeast. Notable features include Sugar Loaf mountain, a smooth granite and quartz mountain next to Rio de Janeiro, and Iguaçu Falls, one of the most spectacular waterfall systems in the world.

The Coastal Lowlands are a small portion of Brazil. Located along the Atlantic coast, they are about 125 miles (200 km) wide in the north and become narrower in the southeast until they recede. By comparison, Brazil is 2,684 miles (4,320 km) from west to east at its widest point.[6] Sandy beaches, coral reefs, and barrier islands make up this area, as well as swamps, floodplains, and lagoons. Craggy mountains sink into the ocean and form the deep harbors of Rio de Janeiro and Salvador.

RIVER SYSTEMS

Several of Brazil's major river systems drain into the Atlantic Ocean. The Amazon River, at about 4,000 miles (6,400 km) long, and its tributaries form the largest of these systems. Running west to east, the Amazon flows from the Andes near Peru into the Atlantic Ocean. Its more than 200 tributaries include the Purus, Madeira, Juruá, Tapajós, and Xingu Rivers, which flow into the Amazon from the south, and the Negro River, which flows into it from the north.[7]

The second-largest river system in Brazil is made up of the combination of the Paraná River and the Paraguay River. The system includes the estuary they flow into. The upper Paraná River begins in south-central Brazil and flows south and then west, picking up many tributaries along the way. The Paraguay River begins in the Pantanal and forms some of Brazil's border with Paraguay before it joins the Paraná. Eventually the Paraná

IGUAÇU FALLS

A UNESCO World Heritage site, Iguaçu Falls is one of the most spectacular waterfall systems in the world. On the border of Brazil and Argentina, the Iguaçu River drops up to 269 feet (82 m) in a set of powerful waterfalls called cataracts.[8] The falls take the shape of a long, skinny horseshoe nearly three times the width of Niagara Falls in the United States. Mist rises high into the sky, creating many rainbows.

MAP OF
BRAZIL

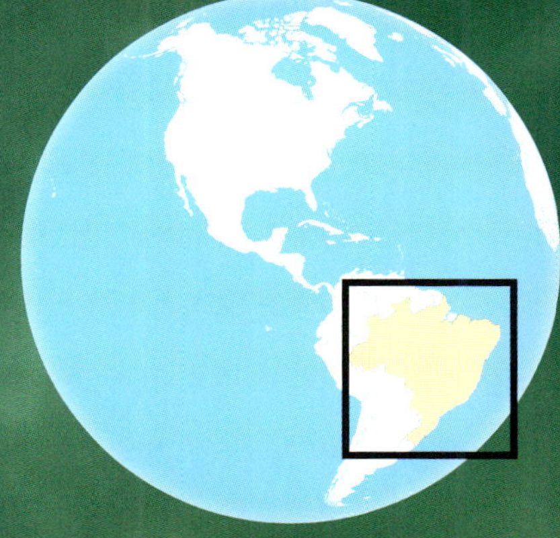

KEY:
- Capital
- City
- Point of Interest

flows out to the Atlantic through an estuary called the Río de la Plata. The Uruguay River, which begins in southern Brazil, also flows into this estuary before emptying into the ocean.

The third-largest river system is made up of the Tocantins River and the Araguaia River. The Tocantins River begins in north-central Brazil, south of the Amazon River. It flows northeast and empties into the Pará River in the Amazon delta. Along the way, it picks up the Araguaia River, which flows north from the Brazilian Highlands.

The São Francisco River is another major river with a large basin. It is the largest river that is completely within Brazil's borders. This river begins in the highlands in eastern Brazil and flows north for hundreds of miles. Eventually it turns east and empties into the Atlantic Ocean.

CLIMATE

The climate in Brazil varies by region. Northern Brazil, which includes the Amazon River basin, has a humid equatorial climate with high temperatures and high humidity throughout the year. The region along the Atlantic coast, from the state of Rio Grande do Norte to the state of São

Brazil's Encontro Das Águas, or "Meeting of the Waters," is where the Solimões and Negro Rivers come together. The contrast between the rivers can be seen at the surface level and from space.

Paulo, experiences a humid tropical climate closer to the equator and a humid subtropical climate farther south. A humid tropical climate has distinct wet and dry seasons with temperatures that remain high all year. A humid subtropical climate also has year-round high temperatures, but with a more even amount of rainfall throughout the year.

The inland state of Mato Grosso, which includes a portion of the Amazon Rain Forest, receives significant precipitation.

Precipitation is lightest in northeast Brazil, which receives 15 to 30 inches (38–76 cm) of rain annually. Much of the country gets heavier

rainfall, totaling 40 to 70 inches (102–178 cm) per year.[9] Parts of the Amazon basin receive even higher amounts than that. Temperatures drop low enough for snowfall only in the southernmost areas of Brazil.

CHAPTER THREE

PLANTS AND ANIMALS

Brazil has some of the most diverse plants and animals on Earth, and they live in six main biomes across the country. A biome is a naturally occurring community of plants and animals that live in the same habitat. Brazil's biomes include the Amazon, Cerrado, Atlantic Forest, Caatinga, Pantanal, and Pampas.

AMAZON

The Amazon biome lies in northern Brazil. It is the largest biome in Brazil and takes up about half its landmass. Its most common ecosystem is its tropical

A vibrant variety of tree frogs call the Amazon biome home.

The massive Brazil nut tree rises to the top layer of the rain forest.

rain forest. However, small areas of savannas, grasslands, swamps, floodplain forests, and palm forests are also present.

Several million species of plants and animals live in the Amazon, making it the most biodiverse place on Earth. About 20 percent of the world's plant species and about 10 percent of all mammals live in the Amazon. In addition, about 1,000 bird species live there, as well as about 1,800 types of butterflies and 2,000 kinds of fish.[1] An estimated 2.5 million species of insects are found in the Amazon too.[2]

The top layer of the rain forest is called the emergent layer, with trees soaring to nearly 200 feet (60 m) in height.[3] Foliage is abundant at the treetops, where leaves experience direct sunlight. In darker areas on the tree trunks below, foliage is less abundant. Many plants in the emergent layer have waxy leaves to hold in water during dry seasons and lightweight seeds that can be carried by the wind. Trees in the emergent layer include the kapok and Brazil nut tree, which can live up to 1,000 years. Most of the animals living in the emergent layer fly or glide; others scamper over thin branches. Animals include birds such as the harpy eagle, white-tailed hawk, and toucan, as well as butterflies and bats.

Below the emergent layer is the canopy. A canopy is a type of covering, like an umbrella. Made of leaves and branches, the rain forest canopy forms a continuous roof about 20 feet (6 m) thick.[4] The canopy blocks out most sunlight, wind, and rain, forming a dark and humid environment. Trees in the canopy have adapted to moist conditions by growing glossy leaves that repel drops of water.

The canopy is home to laurel, palm, acacia, rubber, mahogany, and many other kinds of trees. Bromeliads, a family of tropical plants with sword-shaped leaves, also grow here, as does the liana, a woody vine. With plentiful fruit trees and dense vegetation, the canopy provides reliable food sources for its inhabitants. More animals live in the canopy than in any other layer in the forest. Animals in the canopy layer include tree frogs, spider and howler monkeys, golden lion tamarins, macaws, keel-billed toucans, sloths, and kinkajous, animals that resemble monkeys but are members of the raccoon family. Thousands of insect species live in the canopy, including varieties of bees, beetles, and butterflies.

Below the canopy is the understory. Here, shrubs, bushes, and young trees grow to about 16 feet (5 m) tall.[5] The understory is darker, more humid, and less windy than the canopy. Plants in this area, such as philodendrons and zebra plants, often have large leaves to catch the little

The kinkajou is nocturnal, emerging mainly at night.

sunlight available. Orchids and other plants have bright flowers that attract pollinators such as birds, bees, and bats.

The forest floor is the darkest and lowest layer of the rain forest. Leaves fall to the ground and decay, providing a feast for animals and other organisms. These decomposers break down the decayed material and release nutrients into the soil. Decomposers include slugs, worms, termites, fungi, and scorpions. In turn, larger animals that live on the forest floor, such as armadillos, wild pigs, and anteaters, eat the decomposers. Predatory animals, such as jaguars and leopards, then hunt these animals. Many other animals also live in this area, including small rodents that hide out in the shallow roots of the trees on the Amazon floor and capybaras, which are rodents the size of large dogs.

Plants and animals also live in and around the rivers and lakes of the Amazon River basin. Among them is the anaconda, the largest and heaviest snake in the world. It can weigh more than 550 pounds (249 kg) and measure 30 feet (9 m) long.[6] Amid the many amphibians and reptiles are glass frogs with partially transparent skin, poison dart frogs with bright colors and patterns, and green basilisk lizards that can run on the surface of the water. Manatees, pink river dolphins, piranhas, catfish, and electric eels inhabit the rivers.

> **Less than 10 percent of the sun's rays make it through the canopy of a rain forest.[7]**

OTHER BIOMES

Taking up about one-fifth of Brazil's landmass, the Cerrado biome is in west-central Brazil. In the Cerrado, large swaths of vegetation grow close to the ground. Humid forests grow alongside rivers and creeks. Some of the plants include *pequi*, a type of fruit tree, golden grass, *baru* nut trees, and acai berry trees. Mammals include the maned wolf, giant armadillo, giant anteater, and Brazilian tapir, which has a short trunk-like snout and resembles an elephant, though tapirs are more closely related to horses. Among the biome's birds are the greater rhea, the largest bird in South America, and the red-legged seriema.

The Atlantic Forest biome is mostly along the Atlantic coast. This biome is a tropical rain forest, and it is even older than the Amazon. However, due to development and industry, the forest is now just a tiny portion of its original size. Most of Brazil's population lives in the states of Rio de Janeiro and São Paulo, which lay partially within this biome. Despite its reduced size, large sections of pristine forest remain along the coast. These areas are some of the most biodiverse on Earth and house thousands of unique species of plants.

Like the related ostrich, the greater rhea is a flightless bird.

In addition, the Atlantic Forest has more than 600 amphibian species, including the Brazilian gold frog, the smallest frog in the Southern Hemisphere.[8]

The Caatinga biome is in northeastern Brazil. The Caatinga is dry most of the year with sparse and hardy vegetation, though mountainous areas have more humid air and fertile soil.

The Caatinga is drier than other regions of Brazil, but it still supports a great deal of plant life.

Thorny shrubs, prickly cacti, and leafless trees dot the landscape during dry periods. After rainfall, however, rivers fill with water, green brush covers the ground, and leaves open up on trees. Species unique to this biome include the Lear's macaw, Spix's macaw, and spiny rat.

Located in south-central Brazil, the Pantanal biome covers less than 2 percent of Brazil's landmass.[9] The Pantanal is the largest inland wetland on the planet. Inland wetlands are areas where water covers the soil for part of the year, often in floodplains. During the wet season, rivers overflow and flood most of the land. This creates lakes, marshes, swamps, and islands made of higher ground, changing the landscape dramatically. The floods provide nutrients for the soil, which feeds an abundance of grasses, flowers, scattered trees, and marsh plants called rushes. Wildlife thrives on the rich vegetation and includes thousands of butterflies, such as the orange Julia and light-green cloudless sulphur butterflies; hundreds of fish species, including piranha, *pacu*, and *jau*; and hundreds of birds, such as the heron, ibis, and jabiru stork.

The Pampas biome is a fertile grassland that extends from the Andes Mountains in the west to the Atlantic Ocean in the east. Much of it has been used for cattle ranching, and only a few isolated patches of pristine habitat remain. The plant life in the Pampas includes 400 species of grass. Palm savannas and forests grow in the foothills of the mountains. Some of the 72 species of mammals in this biome include capybaras, pampas deer, and brown brocket deer. Eighty species of birds live in the Pampas region, including the yellow cardinal, greater rhea, and ochre-breasted pipit.[10]

ENVIRONMENTAL ISSUES

Brazil has more than 3,200 plants and animals that are threatened with extinction.[11] *Threatened* is a general term that encompasses species whose status ranges from vulnerable to critically endangered. Many factors are to blame for the decline of these species, including hunting, habitat destruction, and competing animals, such as dogs, rats, lizards, and even humans. The Atlantic

Wide stretches of the Pampas biome are used for grazing cattle and other livestock.

Forest biome is in the worst condition, with about 2,000 threatened species. The Pantanal and Amazon fare the best, with the lowest percentage of threatened species.[13]

Since the late 1700s, Brazil has created more than 1,000 protected areas, biological reserves, and parks to shield the land and its inhabitants.[14] However, many of these places are in remote areas and are hard to maintain. Also, some of the protected lands have been slated for the development of hydroelectric dams, highways, or other construction projects, which would disrupt the land and wildlife.

Deforestation, particularly in the Amazon, threatens the country's plant and animal life. Companies have cut down a significant portion of the Amazon for farming, cattle ranching, and illegal logging. The Brazilian government has planned or started construction on about 30 hydroelectric plants in the Amazon basin.[15] These facilities block the flow of water, which alters watercourses, causing floods and displacing animals and the Indigenous peoples who live there.

Farming doesn't affect only the Amazon. Deforestation in the Pantanal leads to erosion and causes silt to clog rivers. Farmers also use chemicals to help their crops grow. These substances include fertilizers, insecticides, herbicides, and fungicides, which can run off

Aerial photography gives stark evidence of the effect of deforestation on the Amazon biome.

JAGUARS

into the surrounding waters. The chemicals can poison fish and animals and destroy their habitats. These pollutants can also cause algal blooms, where algae grow rapidly on the surface of water. These blooms reduce oxygen levels in the water, making it difficult for aquatic plants to grow and fish to breathe.

CHAPTER FOUR

HISTORY

Archaeological evidence shows that people were living in what is now Brazil 11,000 years ago. People hunted, fished, and gathered food to survive. They developed agriculture and built settlements. Ceramics dating to 7,000 years ago show that Indigenous peoples used ceramics for everyday use, such as storing food and cultural expression. By the 1500s, hundreds of different Indigenous groups lived along the Atlantic coast or inland in the Paraná and Paraguay River basins. Many of these people spoke Tupian languages and shared a similar culture. These Indigenous peoples heavily influenced Brazil's early colonial history and culture. However, the diseases Europeans brought to Brazil wreaked havoc on the Tupian-speaking peoples, and those who survived faced harsh treatment from the Portuguese settlers.

Archaeologists have found rock carvings in Brazil that date back an estimated 4,000 years.

PORTUGUESE ARRIVAL

In 1494, Spain and Portugal established the Treaty of Tordesillas, which divided South America along a vertical line. Everything east of this line would be Portugal's, and everything west of it would be Spain's. Portugal's portion covered the eastern third of what is now Brazil. Spain's portion was the rest of South America. In 1500, the Portuguese king sent a fleet of ships led by Pedro Álvares Cabral to India. Cabral planned on following Vasco da Gama's route around the Cape of Good Hope at the southern tip of Africa. However, Cabral turned west into the Atlantic Ocean to take advantage of winds and currents in that area. He sailed farther west than planned and sighted land along the South American coast. This land was within Portugal's area in the Treaty of Tordesillas, so the Portuguese king claimed it for the country. Because of its abundance of brazilwood trees, the colony was named Brazil.

When the Portuguese and other Europeans landed in Brazil in the early 1500s, they exchanged resources and forged military alliances with Indigenous groups. This European contact became catastrophic for Indigenous communities. What started as an exchange of resources turned

A map from 1502 shows Europeans' significant uncertainty about the shapes of the landmasses in the Americas. It also shows the vertical line, *in blue*, separating Spanish from Portuguese territories in what later became Brazil.

into the Europeans capturing Indigenous people and enslaving them. At the same time, European diseases such as smallpox, tuberculosis, and influenza ravaged Indigenous communities, killing vast numbers of people.

In 1533, the Portuguese divided the colony into 15 captaincies, or inherited estates, that were governed by aristocrats. Two of the captaincies were successful. One was São Vicente, which became present-day São Paulo. The other was Pernambuco, a large sugar-producing region in the northeast that is now the state of the same name. Several years later, the Portuguese king appointed Tomé de Sousa as governor of Brazil. De Sousa named Salvador the capital, placed greater control over the captaincies, and established city governments.

The Portuguese king sent Jesuit missionaries to accompany de Sousa. The goal of the missionaries was to quell tensions with the Indigenous people and convert them to Christianity. Once converted, the Indigenous people could live in Jesuit villages, called *aldeias*, as free people. However, the Jesuits often forced the Indigenous people to convert and then made them work on the Jesuits' cattle ranches and plantations.

In 1550, slave traders began bringing enslaved African people to the port cities of Salvador and Belém. The colonists saw the African people as better workers and more disease-resistant than Indigenous people. They forced the African people to work 17-hour days and live in

A 1665 painting depicts a Jesuit church in northeastern Brazil. Jesuit missionaries came to Brazil in the mid-1500s and pressured Indigenous people to convert to Christianity.

cramped and crowded quarters. As a result, the African people experienced widespread disease and malnutrition.

WESTWARD EXPANSION

As the colony of Brazil expanded westward, expeditions went beyond the line drawn by the Treaty of Tordesillas. Missionaries traveled west along the Amazon and also settled in the south and southeast. Cattle ranchers went inland from the states of Pernambuco and Bahia on the coast, seeking pasture. Ruthless explorers organized expeditions called *bandeiras* looking for Indigenous people to enslave, as well as precious metals and gems.

From the 1500s through the 1700s, the sugar industry provided the most wealth to Brazil, particularly in the northeast. Large landowners ran sugar plantations while smaller farmers produced coffee and cotton. Others raised cattle and grew tobacco. In 1695, Brazilians found gold in the state of Minas Gerais. People flocked from the coast to set up small towns in the uncolonized area near gold sources. Gold brought in a lot of money, so the Portuguese government transferred the colony's capital city from Salvador to Rio de Janeiro, which was closer to the gold mines, in 1763.

During the mid- to late-1700s, after Portuguese expeditions had been moving into and claiming Spanish territory, the two countries signed several treaties giving this land to Portugal. At the same time, Portuguese leader Sebastião José de Carvalho e Mello instituted a series of reforms to unite Brazil and make the colony more profitable. He abolished the system that awarded captaincies, encouraged immigration from Portugal to Brazil, created state-run trading companies, and granted

BANDEIRAS

Bandeiras were Portuguese expeditions into unmapped areas of Brazil, led by *bandeirantes*. They searched for Indigenous people they could enslave and sell. Bandeirantes captured Indigenous people by allying with one tribe and then provoking conflict with another tribe. The bandeirantes would enslave all participants from both tribes.

legal rights to Indigenous peoples. In 1759, he expelled the Jesuits from the Portuguese empire.

INDEPENDENCE AND THE IMPERIAL YEARS

In 1807, Napoléon Bonaparte of France invaded Portugal in order to strengthen the European blockade of the United Kingdom. The prince regent of Portugal, Dom João, and his court escaped to Brazil. Once there, Dom João made Brazil the new seat of the Portuguese government.

Dom João later became King John VI. He returned to Portugal in 1821, and his son, Dom Pedro, took over as prince regent and governor of Brazil. Conflict brewed between the colonists and the Portuguese parliament, as the parliament tried to increase its control over Brazil. It also insisted that Dom Pedro return to Portugal, fearing that he would lead an independence

An illustration from the 1700s depicts the enslaved people who were forced to mine diamonds in Brazil.

MARIA QUITÉRIA DE JESUS

Maria Quitéria de Jesus (1772–1853) grew up in Bahia, Brazil, on a wealthy plantation that her father owned. Her mother died when she was a child, and Quitéria spent most of her time outdoors. She learned to fish, ride horses, and handle weapons. In 1822, the interim council of the Bahia government asked for volunteers to fight for Brazil's independence against Portuguese resistance. Quitéria wanted to enlist, but her father refused to consider it. With the help of her sister and brother-in-law, Quitéria ran away from home. She cut her hair, put on men's clothes, and used her brother-in-law's name to enlist in the army.

Quitéria became known for her discipline, bravery, and skill with weapons. When her father tried to bring her back home, the army did not want to let her go. Since everyone now knew she was a woman, Quitéria changed her name back to her own and added a short skirt to her uniform. Quitéria inspired other women at the time to enlist, and they formed a group led by Quitéria. During the fight to support independence, she stood out as an excellent soldier.

Quitéria received an award from Emperor Pedro I for her performance in battle.

movement in Brazil. Dom Pedro refused, and on June 3, 1822, he assembled a legislative council. On September 7, near São Paulo, he proclaimed Brazil's independence from Portugal. In 1824, the United States recognized Brazilian independence, and a year later, the Portuguese government did too.

The time following independence is known as the imperial period. Two emperors held power during this time. Dom Pedro became Brazil's first emperor, Pedro I. His time in power is significant for the drafting of Brazil's constitution, which went into effect in 1824. Brazil experienced many problems during his rule, including losing a war with Argentina, and Pedro I's popularity declined. He abdicated in 1831 and returned to Europe.

Pedro II became the second emperor upon his father's abdication, but he was just five years old. Assorted advisers helped him run Brazil until he fully took power in 1840. His reign was

Pedro II reigned in Brazil for more than half a century.

successful, but his government intervened in other countries, including invading Uruguay in 1864 to help decide a civil war in favor of a pro-Brazilian government. This disturbed Paraguay, which did not like Brazil expanding its power in the area, so the Paraguayan army marched through Argentina toward Uruguay, which Argentina did not approve. This led to the bloodiest war in South American history. In what was known as the Paraguayan War or the War of the Triple Alliance (1864–1870), Brazil, Argentina, and Uruguay joined forces to fight Paraguay. The alliance eventually destroyed the Paraguayan army, but after the war Brazilian military officers began to question the leadership of the regime.

During Pedro II's reign, Brazil grew in population and economic power. But by the end of his reign, support for Pedro II had weakened, largely due to his antislavery stance. During the 1860s, many colonists, including Pedro II, opposed slavery. But he did not want to anger the slaveholders, who produced sugar and brought wealth to the country. He wanted reform to go slowly. In 1871, the government passed a law abolishing slavery for children whose parents were enslaved. Then in 1884, it passed another law freeing enslaved people who were 60 or older. Finally, in 1888, Princess Isabel, who was acting as regent for Pedro II while he was traveling in Europe, signed a law abolishing all slavery.

Unrest was growing in the country. The wealthy elite supported the monarchy, but the military, middle class, and coffee growers believed the

About 700,000 slaves were freed in 1888 when Princess Isabel emancipated all enslaved people in Brazil.[2]

monarchy was outdated and wanted a representative government. On November 15, 1889, the military staged a coup, and Pedro II abdicated the throne.

MILITARY, DICTATORS, AND DEMOCRACY

The Brazilian military ran the country until the first civilian was elected president in 1894. Prudente de Morais had been the governor of the coffee-growing state of São Paulo, and he was the first in a series of presidents who represented the interests of coffee barons. When the financial crisis of 1929 hit and coffee prices declined, the coffee leaders lost influence. After the 1930 presidential election, the losing Liberal Alliance party led a revolution to place Getúlio Vargas in power. They overthrew the elected president and put Vargas in charge. After a new constitution took effect in 1934, Vargas's temporary presidency ended, and Congress officially elected him as president that same year.

According to the constitution, Vargas would serve a four-year term and then have the opportunity to run for reelection. But Vargas threw out the constitution and made himself dictator in 1937. He jailed his opponents, banned political parties, and censored the press. However, Vargas was popular with workers because he enacted laws that supported labor. In 1942, Brazil entered World War II (1939–1945), declaring war on Germany and Italy and joining the side of the Allies. The United States provided modern military equipment to Brazil, and Vargas sent troops to fight in Italy in 1944. The Allies won the war in 1945. After the war, military leaders feared Vargas would remain in power, so they staged another coup and forced him to resign.

President Juscelino Kubitschek made Brasília the new capital in 1960. This massive change involved major construction projects.

General Eurico Gaspar Dutra, Vargas's former war minister, won the 1945 presidential election and governed for five years. In 1946, the government passed a new constitution. Under its new rules, Vargas would be able to run for president again in 1950. He won the election and promised to follow the new constitution, which limited the president's power. After massive corruption was discovered in the Vargas administration, some army officers demanded he resign. Vargas took his own life on August 24, 1954.

Juscelino Kubitschek de Oliveira won the 1955 election. As president, he instituted many projects to help the economy. He built bridges, highways, and hydroelectric power plants, and he also expanded the production of iron, steel, and oil. Most importantly, on April 21, 1960, he moved the capital to Brasília, well into the interior of the country. This was to encourage development in the region. By the end of Kubitschek's time in office, the country's economy was doing well, but living standards had not improved for most people.

The military took power in 1964, and over the next 20 years five different generals ruled as dictators in a repressive regime. The economy did well during the late 1960s and into the 1970s, and the military tried to institute large construction projects, such as a massive highway through the Amazon. But by the end of the 1970s, the economy declined, and a workers' movement began, which encouraged the generals to move toward a more democratic Brazil. Power passed into civilian hands in 1985. A new constitution, called the "citizen constitution," was drafted with input from public hearings and took effect in 1988.

1990 TO THE 2020s

President Fernando Collor de Mello, elected in 1989, worked to reform consumer laws. However, many scandals led to his impeachment and removal from office. Vice president Itamar Franco took over. His finance minister, Fernando Henrique Cardoso, introduced a financial plan that established a new currency called the *real* (pronounced HAY-ahl). The plan, known as the Real Plan, helped stabilize the Brazilian economy. The real was tied to the US dollar, which prevented the real from being connected to inflation while allowing it to be flexible relative to other currencies. When Cardoso was elected president, inflation fell from nearly 1,000 percent in 1994 to less than 20 percent in 1995 and was almost 0 percent by 1998.[4] With the economy booming, Cardoso was reelected to another term in 1998.

In 2002, a progressive candidate named Luiz Inácio "Lula" da Silva was elected. One of 22 children born to poor farmers, Lula promised to address poverty during his presidency. He became a popular president and ran a financially cautious administration. He instituted antipoverty legislation and helped millions of people rise to the middle class.

Dilma Rousseff was elected as the first female president of Brazil in 2010. During her first term, she dealt with one of the worst natural disasters in Brazilian history when flash floods and mudslides killed approximately 500 people and left thousands more homeless.[5] When Brazil hosted the 2014 World Cup soccer tournament, Rousseff faced protests from people who believed too much had been spent on the World Cup. However, the event was deemed a success, and Rousseff won reelection in 2014. In 2016, Rio de Janeiro hosted the Summer Olympics

The opening ceremony of the 2016 Summer Olympics in Rio was a dramatic celebration of Brazil.

and Paralympics, which helped strengthen Brazil's economy. That same year, though, her administration was accused of corruption, and she was impeached and removed from office.

When conservative candidate and retired captain Jair Bolsonaro ran for election in 2018, he promised to put an end to scandals. Voters were tired of political corruption, and many liked his law-and-order platform. His presidency has been polarizing and controversial. He supported business interests over environmental ones by ignoring illegal logging in the Amazon. Many believed his government did not provide a sufficient response to the spread of COVID-19, which was declared a global pandemic in 2020. The virus led to more than 660,000 deaths in Brazil by June 2022.[6]

PEOPLE AND CULTURE

Modern Brazil is a fusion of peoples and cultures. Starting in the 1500s, the Portuguese brought their language and religion to Brazil. Indigenous peoples and Africans, who were mostly brought over because of the slave trade, added new foods, music styles, and religions to the country. In the late 1800s, millions of Europeans flocked to Brazil to work in coffee fields. Italians, Portuguese, Spaniards, and many others came, bringing their own beliefs and ways of living.

Today Brazil is the seventh-largest country in the world, with a population of more than 217 million.[1] Its largest cities include São Paulo, Minas Gerais,

Rio de Janeiro is the country's second-most populous city, with more than six million residents.

Rio de Janeiro, and Salvador. Brazil's average life expectancy has improved in recent decades, growing from about 66 in 1990 to around 76 in 2022 because of improved living conditions and medical advances.[2] This increased life expectancy, coupled with a decreased birth rate, means that the average age in Brazil is rising.

ETHNIC GROUPS

Brazil was due for a census in 2020, but it was delayed because of the COVID-19 pandemic. According to the previous census completed in 2010, Brazilians of European descent, which includes those with ancestors from Portugal, Italy, Germany, and Spain, made up approximately 48 percent of the population. Those who are of a mixed race—having a combination of Indigenous, European, and African ancestry—comprised about 43 percent of the population. Black people who are not of mixed ancestry were about 8 percent of the population, followed by Asian people at more than 1 percent and Indigenous people at 0.4 percent.[3]

Jewish people first migrated to Brazil in the 1600s, and more came in the 1800s to work in the diamond and rubber industries. White immigrants came mainly from Portugal but also from other countries, especially in the late 1800s and early 1900s. Italians immigrated to the country after Brazil gained independence in 1822. German immigrants came to Brazil in the 1800s and

Afro-Brazilians are Brazilian people with African ancestry. They make up about half of the country's population.

early 1900s. Other people arrived from Spain and Middle Eastern countries in the early 1900s. Japanese immigrants began arriving in Brazil in 1908, particularly to São Paulo to work on coffee plantations.

Brazil has a larger population of people of African descent than any other country in the world outside of Africa. People with African ancestry can be divided into two groups: *pardos*, or people of mixed ethnicities, and *pretos*, or people who are of African heritage and do not have mixed ethnicity. Pretos tend to have a darker skin color and often face more social and economic challenges than other groups. Even though discrimination is illegal, people with darker skin tones experience more violence and intolerance than other groups, especially in areas with more European-descended white people.

In 2010, almost 900,000 Indigenous people lived in Brazil. About 500,000 were in rural areas.[5] The rest lived in and around the country's cities. While Indigenous people can be found throughout the country, most live in northern Brazil, particularly in the Amazon River basin. Many Indigenous groups still live in isolation, and Brazil has the largest number of isolated Indigenous communities in South America.

RELIGION AND LANGUAGE

Roman Catholicism was the official religion in Brazil until 1889. It stayed popular afterward because of the large number of Catholic immigrants who came

Brazil has the largest population of Roman Catholics of any country in the world.

to Brazil in the 1800s and 1900s. In 2010, about two-thirds of the country was Roman Catholic. Less than one-quarter was Protestant, and about 10 percent of the country practiced Buddhism, Shinto, Islam, other religions, or no religion at all. About 2 percent of the country practiced spiritism, a belief that the living can interact with the souls of the dead.[7]

Some people practice religions that combine Christian traditions with Indigenous, African, or spiritist beliefs. Candomblé is one such religion. Brought to Brazil by enslaved Africans, it was officially recognized as a religion in 1976 in the state of Bahia. Candomblé adopted Catholic saints as stand-ins for its own deities in order to hide the religion from slaveholders.

Even though Portuguese is the official language of Brazil, it has changed over the years and is different from what is spoken in Portugal, in terms of both the pronunciations and meanings of words. One reason is that immigrants from Italy, Germany, Japan, and Spanish-speaking countries have introduced words and phrases into Brazil that are now commonplace. For instance, the Italian word for goodbye, *ciao*, is now used in Brazil, though it is spelled *tchau*. In addition, the Tupian languages of certain Indigenous peoples were the main way of communicating in the early days of colonization. Brazilian Portuguese includes words from these languages. Some experts believe this led to the biggest divergence between the Portuguese languages used in Brazil and Portugal.

THE ARTS

During the 1700s, Brazilian artists began developing Western styles of painting. In the 1800s, the Imperial Academy of Fine Arts in Brazil was a big influence on the art world. It trained artists, organized exhibitions, and curated art collections that specialized in historical scenes and landscapes. In the late 1800s, the painter Belmiro de Almeida moved to more intimate and realistic scenes of daily life. A uniquely Brazilian way of painting was developed in the 1900s by Cândido Portinari. He mixed realistic portraits of Brazilians with abstract European techniques to create

A painting depicting a couple's argument is Belmiro de Almeida's most popular work.

art about the inequality between the wealthy and the people who work for them. In 1952, the Brazilian government commissioned him to paint a two-panel mural called *War and Peace* to be displayed in the United Nations headquarters in the United States. One panel depicts the horrors of World War II using purple and red tones, while the other portrays peace after war in yellow tones. The murals still hang there.

Brazil has produced many world-renowned authors throughout the centuries. In the 1800s, Joaquim Maria Machado de Assis, the son of a former slave, was known for his Romantic novels. In the 1900s, many writers came from the northeastern area of the country. Gilberto de Mello Freyre wrote about life under slavery, while João Guimarães Rosa wrote stories about violence and survival in the interior of the country. Brazil's most famous author is Jorge Amado, known for his colorful romances set in Bahia's cacao-growing region. Clarice Lispector was considered one of the greatest novelists in Latin America in the 1900s. She wrote about human isolation and moral doubt. Popular novelist Paulo Coelho wrote the best-selling 1988 novel *The Alchemist*, which has been translated into 80 languages.[8]

JORGE AMADO

Jorge Amado grew up on a cacao plantation in the state of Bahia. His early writing dealt with life on plantations, and he wrote about the way migrant Black people, mixed-race people, and poor white people were exploited. Amado became active in communist politics, and he was jailed in 1935 as part of a government crackdown on people deemed antigovernment. He continued to write about Bahian city life into the 1990s.

ARCHITECTURE

When the Portuguese first came to Brazil, their focus was on practicality and survival. Dwellings were made of wood and earth, while stone citadels and fortresses guarded the coast. The Jesuits built missions, especially in Rio Grande do Sul, with brick exteriors and baroque details, such as twists and curves, bright colors, gilded sculptures, and dramatic facades. The interiors featured carved wood decorations.

Geometric facades adorned the earliest colonial buildings. Later, as coffee brought wealth to the country, architects designed churches in the baroque style with carved, gold-leafed interiors. Salvador has many examples of this. Designers constructed buildings in Rio de Janeiro with a neoclassical form, featuring elongated columns and wide domes. By the 1930s, art deco had become popular, with its geometric shapes and lack of ornamentation.

Geometric buildings with long rows of windows are common in Salvador.

Oscar Niemeyer, perhaps Brazil's most famous architect, ushered in an era of modernism. In the 1950s, Niemeyer worked with urban planner Lúcio Costa and landscape architect Roberto Burle Marx to design Brasília. This planned city is known for its unusual street layout, which is in the shape of an airplane, as well as iconic buildings, such as a cathedral in the shape of a crown.

MUSIC

Brazilian music has had many influences, ranging from the rattlers, shakers, and panpipes played by Indigenous peoples to the drumming used by enslaved Africans and the melodic ballads sung by the Portuguese. Even European dance musical styles in the 1800s, such as the polka and mazurka, contributed to the mix. All of these sounds created the rich tapestry of modern Brazilian music.

It wasn't until the samba that Brazilian music found its sound. Samba originated in a Rio de Janeiro neighborhood in the early 1900s. It combined distinct rhythms, using percussive instruments, with simple harmonies and an emphasis on melody. Today, samba is often associated

Members of the Vila Isabel samba school performed at the Rio Carnival parade in 2014.

with Carnival, an extravagant festival featuring numerous parades and street parties with colorful floats, live samba music, and dancers in sequined costumes.

Samba isn't only a type of music—it is also a type of dance. Dating back to the 1500s, samba dancing began with Congolese and Angolan circle dancing and involved rotating hip movements. Brazilian slaveholders didn't approve of the dancing, so samba was mainly done in private. After slavery was abolished, the dancing moved to favelas around Rio de Janeiro, and as samba music took shape, the dance of samba became more popular. Today, this dance, with its origin in African rhythms, is a symbol of cultural identity in Brazil.

Bossa nova music emerged in the late 1950s. Bossa nova is a slower version of samba with a harmonic style, attractive melodies, and quiet lyrics. The founders of this new genre included Antônio Carlos "Tom" Jobim, guitarist João Gilberto, and lyricist Vinícius de Moraes. Bossa nova reflected the optimistic mood of the country.

FOOD

Brazil's varied landscape provides a wide range of fresh produce and proteins. Tropical fruits and vegetables from the rain forests, large fish from the Amazon River, and steaks from cattle ranches are part of the cuisine. Traditional dishes combine Portuguese and African elements. A staple of most diets is farinha, a combination of rice, beans, and dried ground manioc. Churrasco, a type of grilled meat, is popular throughout the country. Along the coast and in the northeast, seafood is common, such as a fish stew called *peixe a Brasileira*. On the dinner plates in the country's interior

Brazilian food combines influences from the nation's diverse cultures with the land's bountiful crops.

is *carne seca* or *carne de sol*, which consists of beef or goat served with squash. The Amazon Rain Forest provides dishes prepared with *tucupi*, a sauce made from manioc root that numbs the tongue. A snack called *salgadinhos*, cheese- or meat-filled fried dough, is a popular appetizer. Desserts, such as the coconut custard *quindim*, are usually sweet and made with fruit.

POLITICS

Brazil's official name is the Federative Republic of Brazil, and it has a federal presidential republic type of government. A federal form of government is one in which power is divided between the national government and smaller state and municipal governments. A presidential republic is a government with a president leading an executive branch that is separate from other governmental branches. Like the United States, Brazil has executive, legislative, and judicial branches of government.

EXECUTIVE BRANCH

The president is both head of state and head of government. As head of state, the president represents the country to the world. As head of government, the president runs the executive branch. The president

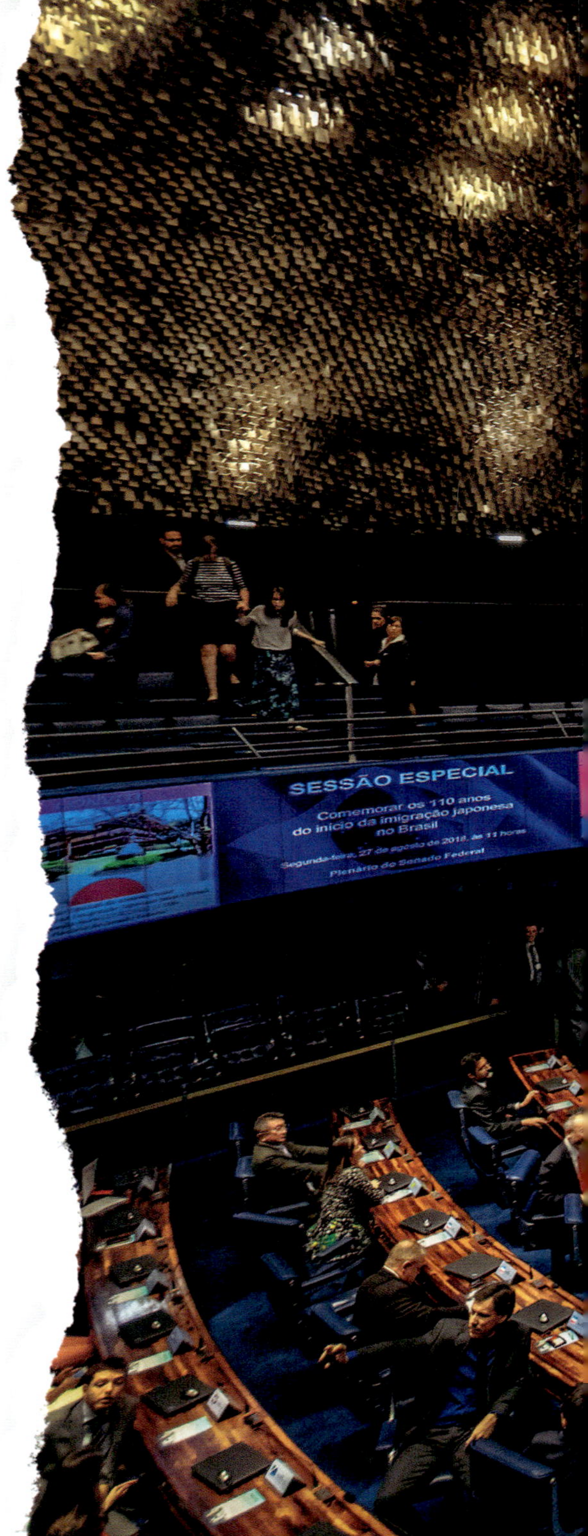

The Brazilian National Congress meets throughout the entire year, with recesses in January and at the end of July.

President Jair Bolsonaro was elected in 2018.

also leads the armed forces. Unlike in the United States, where only the legislative branch writes bills, the Brazilian president can draft and submit bills to Congress. Congress must vote to approve or reject the bill within 30 days. If it fails to vote on the bill, the bill is automatically passed. When the legislature sends a bill to the president, the president can fully or partially approve the bill or veto it.

Presidential terms last four years, and presidents can serve two terms total. Presidents and vice presidents run on the same ballot and must win by an absolute majority, with more votes than all the other candidates combined. If there is no absolute majority after the first round of ballots, then a second round is called.

Presidents appoint cabinet members. Cabinet members are ministers of state and other heads of departments. The cabinet includes 23 ministers, including chief of staff, minister of foreign affairs, minister of justice, defense minister, minister of health, and secretary of government, among others.[1] The president can replace a cabinet member at any time and for any reason.

LEGISLATIVE BRANCH

Brazil's legislative branch consists of the National Congress. It is bicameral, meaning it has two houses. These are the Federal Senate and the Chamber of Deputies. The Federal Senate has 81 members who serve eight-year terms. They are elected directly by a simple majority. There are three senators for each of the 26 states and for the Federal District. The Chamber of Deputies has 513 members. The number of seats is proportional to the population. The greater the population of a state, the more deputies it has. Each state is limited to a maximum of 70 deputies, with a minimum of eight. This results in overrepresentation for less populated states in the north and northeast and underrepresentation for states that are more populated, such as São Paulo. Deputies serve four-year terms and are directly elected by a simple majority.

In 2022, women comprised 17 percent of the Federal Senate and 15 percent of the Chamber of Deputies.[2]

Brazil's National Congress has many powers granted by the constitution. It can pass laws on issues involving the federal government, especially fiscal policies, such as how public funds

Famous architect Oscar Niemeyer designed the Brazilian National Congress building in Brasília.

are spent. It authorizes international treaties and allows the president to declare wars. If the president vetoes a congressional bill, the National Congress has 30 days to override the veto by an absolute majority vote.

JUDICIAL BRANCH

Brazil's justice system is divided into ordinary and special branches. The ordinary branch has both state and federal courts that hear civil and criminal cases. The special branch hears specific types of cases. This branch includes military courts that hear cases involving the armed forces; labor courts that hear cases involving labor disputes between management and workers; and electoral courts that register political parties, pick dates for elections, and hear cases on electoral crime.

The Supreme Federal Court is the highest court in the land. It has 11 justices who are nominated by the president and approved by the Federal Senate. The Supreme Federal Court rules mostly on constitutional issues, but it also hears cases involving government officials, such as the president, the vice president, and members of the legislature and judiciary. Below the Supreme Federal Court is the Higher Court of Justice. This court hears cases that involve state and Federal District governors. This court has 33 justices who are nominated by the president and approved by the Federal Senate.

MAJOR REGIONS

Brazil's government has divided the country into five regions, called the Major Regions. This was done to help the federal, state, and local governments distribute money and implement policies. The regions are the North, Northeast, Southeast, South, and Central-West.

The North is the largest region geographically but has a smaller population and economy than some other regions. Seven of Brazil's states lie within this area. The Amazon Rain Forest covers much of the North. The Northeast is made up of nine states and the island of Fernando de Noronha. Its largest city is Salvador. This region borders the Atlantic Ocean and was the first region in Brazil colonized by Europeans.

The Southeast contains four states. Compared to other regions, the Southeast covers a small area. However, the Southeast is home to the most people of all of Brazil's major regions. It includes major cities, such as Rio de Janeiro, São Paulo, and Minas Gerais. The South is the smallest region in area and has just three states. However, about 14 percent of Brazil's population lives in the South. The Central-West contains three states and the Federal District. Brasília is in the Federal District, and it has a population of 4.8 million.[3]

STATE AND MUNICIPAL GOVERNMENTS

Brazil has 26 states plus the Federal District, which operates like the states. The states have some independence from the federal government. Run by directly elected governors, the states have their own legislatures, justice systems, and constitutions. The largest states by population are São Paulo, Minas Gerais, and Rio de Janeiro. In addition, the largest cities are often the state capitals and share the same name. For instance, São Paulo is the capital of the state of São Paulo. And Rio de Janeiro is the capital of the state of Rio de Janeiro.

States are divided into municipalities. These are geographic areas within each state, similar to counties in the United States. They have independent governments with municipal councillors, directly elected mayors, and their own sources of funds. Some of their responsibilities include road construction, primary education, and the building and maintenance of parks and museums. Municipalities are further divided into districts.

POLITICAL PARTIES

Brazil has a multiparty system. In 2018, 35 parties registered for the elections, and people from 30 different parties won seats in the Chamber of Deputies.[4] The diverse range of parties can make it difficult for the executive branch to fill jobs, as elected officials have varied ideological positions. Among the newest political parties is the União Brasil. It is a combination of the Democratas and the Social Liberal Party.

Another major party is the Workers' Party. This liberal party was created to oppose the military dictatorship and promote social welfare. Presidents Lula and Rousseff were elected as members of this party. Until the formation of União Brasil, the Party of the Brazilian Democratic Movement was the largest, and it held the most seats in Congress in 2016. Like the Workers' Party, it was formed to

The Workers' Party in Brazil faced backlash in 2016, with demonstrators protesting the party's growing number of corruption scandals.

oppose military rule. It began as a moderate liberal party but has members who are more deeply conservative too. The Brazilian Social Democratic Party is a center-left party and a rival to the Workers' Party. It supports social justice, environmentalism, and land reform.

CONSTITUTION

Brazil has had eight constitutions since its independence in 1822. Congress ratified the most recent constitution in 1988. It gave many powers to the federal government while allowing the states to remain partially self-governing. The new constitution described the functions of the three branches of government, set restrictions on the president's power to make laws, and removed any ability of the military to run the government as it had in the past. The constitution allowed the federal government to intervene in state and local issues, and it set the voting age to 16.

The constitution has been amended almost every year. The process begins with a proposal for a new amendment made by at least one-third of the Federal Senate or Chamber of Deputies. Proposals can also come from a majority vote in more than half of the states' legislatures. For an amendment to be passed, a three-fifths majority of both houses of Congress must approve the amendment. Items that cannot be amended include voting rights, separation of powers, individual rights, and anything affecting the federal structure of government.

WOMEN IN THE BRAZILIAN NAVY

In 1980, Brazil integrated women into the navy with the Women's Auxiliary Navy Reserve. They were able to work in administrative, health, and technical areas. In 2012, the navy was the first of the Brazilian armed forces to promote a woman to general officer rank. And in 2018, a female rear admiral was promoted from the corps of engineers. In 2020, women made up about 11 percent of the navy.[7] They can now work in areas that used to allow only men.

ARMED FORCES

Brazil has the largest military in South America, with about 360,000 active personnel.[6] The president is the commander in chief. The focus of the armed forces is mainly on border patrol, especially in the northern Amazon states. The branches of the military are the army, navy, and air force. All men 18 to 45 years of age must participate in military service lasting up to a year. Women are excluded from this requirement, though they have been allowed to enlist in the army since the 1980s, and in 2021, they were allowed to enlist in the combat force of the marine corps.

CHAPTER SEVEN

ECONOMICS

Brazil has the eighth-largest economy in the world, with a gross domestic product (GDP) of $1.61 trillion.[1] GDP is the total value of the goods and services produced by a country in a year. About 72.7 percent of Brazil's GDP comes from the service sector, which includes hospitality and tourism. Industry, including manufacturing and chemical processing for materials such as petroleum, makes up about 20.7 percent of GDP. Agriculture from coffee, soybeans, and other products is 6.6 percent of GDP.[2]

Brazil's official currency has been the real since 1994. A real can be divided into 100 centavos. The Brazilian currency includes real coins, which come in denominations of one, five, ten, 25, and 50 centavos

Brazil is the leading coffee producer in the world.

and a one-real coin. The country also has bills of two, five, ten, 20, 50, and 100 reais. *Reais* is the plural of real.

NATURAL RESOURCES

Brazil's natural resources, both renewable and nonrenewable, are an important part of the economy. Renewable resources, such as timber and fish, are naturally replaced. Nonrenewable resources, such as oil and gas, cannot be replaced. Because Brazil is strong in manufacturing, many of its nonrenewable minerals and ores go directly to its factories. This includes extremely rich deposits of iron ore, copper, tin, and bauxite, the mineral that aluminum comes from. Brazil also has large quantities of granite, manganese, kaolin, and tantalum, which all have industrial uses.

Most of Brazil's petroleum and natural gas reserves are found offshore. Much of its petroleum comes from the continental shelf near Rio de Janeiro. The states of Bahia and Sergipe contain much of the country's natural gas. The Amazon basin also contains reserves of both petroleum and natural gas.

The state-run gas company Petrobras, headquartered in Rio de Janeiro, operates thousands of oil and gas wells off the coast of Brazil.

Brazil has an abundance of timber from the vast forests that cover a large part of the country. Most of the timber comes from the South and Southeast and includes eucalyptus trees, Honduras pine, and other species. These trees are made into paper products and cellulose, which can be used for many goods.

Seafood is another renewable resource. In the Northeast, the saltwater catch consists of lobsters and shrimp. One-quarter of all fish caught in Brazil are freshwater species, mostly from the Amazon River basin. The Northeast has reservoirs stocked with tilapia. To help develop the fishing industry, the Brazilian government spent $700 million in 2022 for additional fishing ports, which

Cattle ranches cover a large swath of Brazil's countryside.

will help as many as 59,000 people who work in the industry.[3]

Brazil generates most of its electricity from renewable sources of power. Hydroelectric power—electricity generated from running water—supplied 66 percent of all electricity in Brazil in 2020. Wind and solar power provided 11 percent of Brazil's electricity, and biomass, which uses organic material as fuel, accounted for 8 percent of electricity. Nonrenewable fossil fuels, such as natural gas, provided 12 percent of electricity.[4] By 2030, the Brazilian government plans for most of its new power generation to use renewable energy sources.

AGRICULTURE AND LIVESTOCK

In 2020, Brazil was ranked fourth in the world in food production.[5] Agriculture and livestock are a vital part of Brazil's economy. Brazil produces more coffee than any other country. Coffee is grown in several areas of Brazil, and the taste varies depending on where it is grown. Brazil is also the world leader in soybeans. Along with the products made from them, soybeans bring in even more revenue than coffee. Other important crops include oranges, cassava, beans, corn, cacao, bananas, and rice. Most Brazilian farmers have small plots of land and rely on manual labor to harvest crops. Larger farms in the South and Southeast use tractors and other expensive farm machinery.

Brazil is one of the world's leaders in meat production. Brazil has roughly the same number of cows as it does people.[6] Most grazing land for cattle lies in the South and Southeast, with smaller areas in the northern parts of the country. Brazil is the largest exporter of poultry meat in the world.[7]

MANUFACTURING AND SERVICE

Brazil plays an important global role in several manufacturing sectors. It is one of the world's largest suppliers of automobiles. Textiles have been a major industry in Brazil since the early 1880s, and they remain so today. Other industries include electrical machinery, paints, soaps, medicines, chemicals, steel, and food. Manufacturing is centered in the Southeast, which has a diverse collection of large factories. The Southeast employs about 60 percent of Brazil's manufacturing

Brazil is a major center for vehicle manufacturing, including cars, trucks, buses, and farm machinery.

workforce, and the South employs about 20 percent.[8] Most other industrial workers are in the North.

The service industry accounts for more than half of the jobs in Brazil. Most service work in the private sector is in retail sales and personal services. Other service work includes employment in hotels, restaurants, bars, and small businesses such as repair shops. Public service work for the government may involve work for public utilities or for government departments and agencies at the federal, state, or local level.

Tourism is a growing industry. Most tourists flock to Rio de Janeiro and other urban centers with plenty of hotels, restaurants, and other hospitality services. The cities of Salvador and Bahia and the coastal areas in the Northeast are also popular. Many people enjoy ecotourism in the Amazon. Tourists like to visit natural wonders such as Iguaçu Falls, beaches, national parks, and historic sites.

TRANSPORTATION

For much of Brazil's history, the coastal areas had reliable transportation via ships and small roads,

Brazil's extensive coastline provides many places for cargo ships to load and unload imports and exports.

but the interior remained mostly isolated. Railroads were built in the 1800s to help bring minerals to ports. After World War II, air travel developed, and Brazil boasted the third-largest commercial air fleet in the world by the 1970s.[10] During the 1990s, the country also built a modern road network. Today, all major cities are connected by roads, including cities in parts of the Amazon. Most people and cargo travel by road.

The majority of Brazil's ships sail from the coast, carrying imports and exports. Petrobras, the government-run oil company, controls most coastal shipping. Brazilians also travel on the country's approximately 31,000 miles (50,000 km) of navigable rivers.[11] In the North, this is the main way of travel, and many boats sail along the Amazon River and its tributaries. Some barges, flat-bottomed cargo vessels designed for rivers and canals, sail down the Paraguay and Paraná Rivers to the Atlantic. However, only 5 percent of cargo is transported via inland waterways.[12]

Brazil has three major airlines. Every major city has an airport, and most smaller towns and cities have airstrips. Rio de Janeiro and São Paulo can accommodate international flights.

CHAPTER EIGHT

BRAZIL TODAY

The experience of living in Brazil depends on a person's ethnicity and social class. In general, those with darker skin are disadvantaged both economically and socially, while lighter-skinned people and European descendants are part of the upper classes. There is a large gap between the rich and the poor.

Family is a big part of Brazilians' lives, and it's common for multiple generations to live under one roof. Friends, teachers, and others are often considered part of the family too. Husbands are the head of the house and work outside the home, and even when wives have jobs, they perform most of the

Many Brazilians' homes include the nuclear family unit and extended relatives.

household duties. This reflects Brazil's long tradition as a patriarchal society, where men hold most of the power in private and public businesses. However, women have been entering the workforce in greater numbers, and in 2022, they held up to 43 percent of jobs.[1]

EDUCATION

In Brazil, schooling is mandatory until 17 years of age. School must be in session for at least 200 days, with the school year lasting from February to December with a winter break in July. Portuguese is spoken in all schools. The constitution gives Indigenous peoples the right to be taught in their own language, but only a few schools have accommodated this so far. One of those is for Mbyá Guaraní children who live outside São Paulo in Tekoa Pyau, a village of about 700 Indigenous people.[2]

Children ages four to five must go to preschool, which could be day care or kindergarten, for two years. Starting at age six, children attend elementary school, which is first through

Some Brazilian boys in favelas receive soccer coaching as a part of their education. Through the Pirelli Inter Campus program, students get to wear the jerseys of the famous Inter Milan team as long as they continue their education.

ninth grade. Elementary school is broken up into two cycles. For the first cycle of five years, students stay in one classroom and have one teacher all day. In the second cycle, they have a variety of teachers. Subjects include geography, natural science, Portuguese, math, physical education, and history. English is required starting in sixth grade.

High school begins right after elementary school. It lasts three years, covering tenth through 12th grade. If students complete elementary school, they can usually go straight into high school, but some high schools require them to take an entrance exam. High school subjects include math, physics, chemistry, biology, history, social studies, and more. Instead of regular high school, students have the option to go to military, technical, or teacher-training schools.

Only a small portion of Brazilians go to colleges or universities. Traditionally, these institutions were only for the rich or some in the middle class. Limited space in free public universities restricted their enrollment to just the top students. This led the way for private colleges to flourish. In 2019, about 88 percent of all higher education institutions in Brazil were private.[4] Most colleges are in the South and Southeast. The largest public university and private school are both in São Paulo state: the University of São Paulo and Paulista University.

SPORTS AND RECREATION

For recreation, Brazilians enjoy being outdoors, either at the beach or a park, picnicking and playing sports. Young people go dancing in nightclubs in the cities, and many families flock to malls for shopping. Soccer, known as *futebol* in Brazil, is by far the most popular sport. People of all ages enjoy playing and watching it. There are hundreds of

FLAMENGO SOCCER CLUB

First founded in 1895 as a rowing team, Flamengo is the most successful soccer team in Brazil. It didn't start out that way. Its record in the first half of the 1900s was unremarkable, but in the 1970s, the team won many championships in Brazil, which began a golden era for the team. In 2019, it set a new team record for an undefeated streak, going 24 matches without losing.[5]

PELÉ

Edson Arantes do Nascimento, also known as Pelé, grew up in poverty. He learned how to play soccer by kicking an old sock stuffed with rags. Seeing his talent, a former member of the Brazilian national team invited Pelé to join a youth squad. The coach persuaded Pelé's parents to let 15-year-old Pelé leave home and try out for the Santos Football Club in the state of São Paulo. His parents agreed, and soon, Pelé led the team in goals.

The Brazilian national team recruited Pelé to join them and play in the 1958 World Cup in Sweden. At just 17 years old, Pelé scored three goals in the semifinals and two more goals in the finals to bring the championship to Brazil. Pelé immediately became a worldwide star, and many countries offered him big contracts. After being declared a national treasure, Pelé chose to stay in Brazil. Due to injuries, he wasn't able to play in the 1962 or 1966 World Cups, but he came back in 1970 to score four goals and give Brazil the championship once again. Pelé retired briefly before playing for the New York Cosmos until 1977. Since then, Pelé has served as Brazil's Extraordinary Minister for Sport and a United Nations ambassador for the environment.

In 2022, Pelé remained the top goal-scorer for Brazil with 77 goals for the national team.

Brazil's men's national soccer team won gold on their home turf during the 2016 Summer Olympics. The men's team placed first again in the 2020 Olympics.

professional clubs in the country. The Brazil men's national team is usually a top contender in the World Cup, the international tournament that occurs once every four years with 32 national teams competing. Many world-famous soccer stars have come from Brazil, including Pelé and Marta.

Volleyball is Brazil's second-most-popular sport, especially after the men's team won the gold medal at the 1992 Olympics in Barcelona and then another gold on home soil at the

Rio de Janeiro Olympics in 2016. Beach volleyball is also big, and thousands of fans turn out to watch championships. Car racing became popular when Brazil won several Formula One championships. Brazil does well in the Olympic sports of track and field, yachting, soccer, volleyball, basketball, and swimming. When the Summer Olympics were held in Rio de Janeiro in 2016, Brazil became the first country in South America to host the games.

FESTIVALS AND HOLIDAYS

Brazil's national holidays include Easter, Christmas, New Year's Day, and Labor Day. Brazil also has some unique holidays. Indian Day is celebrated on April 19 in states with large Indigenous populations, such as Mato Grosso do Sul, Mato Grosso, Pará, and Goiás. Tiradentes Day on April 21 commemorates the execution of Joaquim José da Silva Xavier, also known as Tiradentes, who died while fighting for Brazilian independence in the late 1700s. Our Lady of Aparecida Day is celebrated on October 12 to honor Brazil's patron saint, Virgin Mary Aparecida. And Republic Proclamation Day on November 15 acknowledges the military coup of 1889 that ended the reign of Pedro II.

The biggest holiday is Carnival, which begins the Friday afternoon before Ash Wednesday. Ash Wednesday is a Catholic holy day that begins a time of prayer and preparation for Easter. Rio de Janeiro's Carnival celebration is the most famous, but Salvador, Recife, and Olinda also have large Carnival festivals.

CHALLENGES FOR THE FUTURE

The spread of COVID-19 began in late 2019 and was declared a pandemic in early 2020. In many countries, schools and businesses shut down and hospitals became overrun with patients. Brazil responded by declaring a health emergency and urging states to put social-distancing policies in place to help prevent the spread of the virus. In ten months, Brazil had more than 200,000 deaths from COVID-19.[6] As case counts dropped later in 2020, restrictions eased for a while, and people began heading back to restaurants and tourist attractions. However, when new variants of the virus caused cases to rise, President Bolsonaro did not reinstate restrictive measures. He urged workers to keep working. Bolsonaro's response to the pandemic infuriated many Brazilians.

By June 2022, Brazil had reported more than 31 million cases of COVID-19.[7]

Mourners attended a mass burial of deceased COVID-19 victims on May 19, 2020, in Manaus, Brazil.

By mid-2022, with the increased availability of vaccines, about 86 percent of Brazilians had received at least one dose.[8] At the same time, with virus case counts falling, the economy began returning to prepandemic levels. But unemployment and poverty rates were high. Inflation was also rising, which caused prices of goods and services to rise.

Brazil has weathered many challenges over a history lasting thousands of years. It has experienced colonization, revolution, political upheaval, and a worldwide pandemic. And even though it has work to do to address its current problems, the strength of its people will help Brazil face the future.

ESSENTIAL FACTS

OFFICIAL NAME: FEDERATIVE REPUBLIC OF BRAZIL

GEOGRAPHY

Area: 3,287,957 square miles (8,515,770 sq km)

Highest Elevation: Neblina Peak at 9,888 feet (3,014 m)

Lowest Elevation: Atlantic Ocean at 0 feet (0 m)

PEOPLE

Population: 217.2 million (2022 est.)

Most Populous City: São Paulo (22.4 million)

Ethnic Groups: White, mixed, Black, Asian, Indigenous

Religions: Roman Catholicism, Protestantism, other forms of Catholicism and Christianity, spiritism, other

GOVERNMENT

Type of Government: Federal presidential republic

Capital: Brasília

Head of State and Government: President

Legislature: Bicameral, with a Federal Senate and Chamber of Deputies

ECONOMY

Currency: Real

Major Industries: Agriculture, textiles, chemicals, lumber, minerals, natural gas, machinery and equipment

Natural Resources: Bauxite, gold, iron ore, manganese, platinum, tin, rare earth elements, petroleum, hydropower, timber

NATIONAL SYMBOLS

National Anthem: "Hino Nacional Brasileiro" ("Brazilian National Anthem")

National Bird: Rufous-bellied thrush

National Flower: Ipê-amarelo

GLOSSARY

ABDICATE
To give up power or office.

BIODIVERSE
Having many different plants and animals in an ecosystem.

CONTINENTAL SHELF
A shallow underwater plain of varying width that borders a continent and ends with a steep drop to the ocean floor.

COUP
An attempt to overthrow government leaders.

ESTUARY
An area where river water meets seawater.

FLOODPLAIN
Land adjacent to a river that is subject to flooding.

INFLATION
An increase in the price of goods and services.

MUNICIPALITY

A primary urban political unit, usually with powers of self-government.

NEOCLASSICAL

Relating to a revival or adaptation of the classical era, especially in literature, art, or architecture.

PATRIARCHAL

Characteristic of a system of society or government in which men are dominant.

RATIFY

To formally approve or adopt an idea or document.

SAVANNA

A treeless plain.

SPECIES

A group of organisms that are very similar and can breed with each other.

TRIBUTARY

A stream or river feeding a larger stream, river, or lake.

SELECTED BIBLIOGRAPHY

Balkovich, Robert, et al. *Brazil*. Lonely Planet, 2019.

Burns, E. Bradford, et al. "Brazil." *Encyclopedia Britannica*, 21 Mar. 2022, britannica.com. Accessed 2 June 2022.

Pickard, Christopher. *Insight Guide: Brazil*. Insight Guides, 2019.

FURTHER READINGS

Allen, John. *Growing Up in Brazil*. ReferencePoint Press, 2018.

Hand, Carol. *Bringing Back Our Tropical Forests*. Abdo, 2018.

Pelleschi, Andrea. *Amazon Explorers*. Abdo, 2020.

ONLINE RESOURCES

To learn more about Brazil, please visit **abdobooklinks.com** or scan this QR code. These links are routinely monitored and updated to provide the most current information available.

MORE INFORMATION

For more information on this subject, contact or visit the following organizations:

Afro-Brazilian Museum of the Federal University of Bahia
Largo do Terreiro de Jesus s/n
Building of the Faculty of Medicine of Bahia 40026-010
Historic Center Salvador, Bahia, Brazil
mafro.ceao.ufba.br
This museum has extensive collections of African and African-Brazilian wood carvings, pottery, and other artifacts with Brazilian and African artistic traditions.

Paço Imperial
Praça XV de Novembro, 48
Centro – Rio de Janeiro
amigosdopacoimperial.org.br
The Paço Imperial, or Imperial Palace, was the home of Dom João and his family when they fled from Portugal to Brazil. The palace is open for tours and has exhibitions.

US Embassy in Brazil
SES – Av. Das Nações, Quadra 801, Lote 03
70403-900 – Brasília, DF
br.usembassy.gov
The US Embassy in Brazil provides all kinds of services for US citizens, including safety, travel, and cultural information.

SOURCE NOTES

CHAPTER 1. A TOUR OF BRAZIL
1. "History of Brazil." *Encyclopedia Britannica*, n.d., britannica.com. Accessed 7 July 2022.
2. "12 Best Things to Do in Rio de Janeiro." *US News*, 12 Apr. 2021, travel.usnews.com. Accessed 7 July 2022.
3. "Mount Corcovado." *Encyclopedia Britannica*, 20 June 2016, britannica.com. Accessed 7 July 2022.
4. Lorraine Murray. "Christ the Redeemer." *Encyclopedia Britannica*, 14 Aug. 2021, britannica.com. Accessed 7 July 2022.
5. Susan L. Woodward. "Amazon Rainforest." *Biomes of the World*, 2019, php.radford.edu. Accessed 7 July 2022.

CHAPTER 2. GEOGRAPHY
1. "Brazil." *CIA World Factbook*, 1 July 2022, cia.gov. Accessed 7 July 2022.
2. E. Bradford Burns et al. "Brazil." *Encyclopedia Britannica*, 1 Aug. 2022, britannica.com. Accessed 7 July 2022.
3. James J. Parsons et al. "Amazon River." *Encyclopedia Britannica*, 28 Jan. 2021, britannica.com. Accessed 7 July 2022.
4. "Neblina Peak." *Encyclopedia Britannica*, 7 July 2017, britannica.com. Accessed 7 July 2022.
5. Parsons et al., "Amazon River," *Encyclopedia Britannica*.
6. "Brazil - Locations, Size, and Extent." *Nations Encyclopedia*, 2022, nationsencyclopedia.com. Accessed 7 July 2022.
7. "Maps of Brazil." *World Atlas*, 25 Feb. 2021, worldatlas.com. Accessed 7 July 2022.
8. "Iguaçu Falls." *Encyclopedia Britannica*, 5 Sept. 2019, britannica.com. Accessed 7 July 2022.
9. "Climate of Brazil." *Encyclopedia Britannica*, n.d., britannica.com. Accessed 7 July 2022.
10. "The Climate in Brazil." *World Data*, n.d., worlddata.info. Accessed 13 July 2022.

CHAPTER 3. PLANTS AND ANIMALS

1. Robert Balkovich et al. *Brazil*. Lonely Planet, 2019. 2155.

2. "Insects Kick Biomass." *Nature and Culture International*, 2022, natureandculture.org. Accessed 7 July 2022.

3. "Rainforest." *National Geographic*, n.d., education.nationalgeographic.org. Accessed 4 Aug. 2022.

4. "Rainforest," *National Geographic*.

5. Balkovich et al., *Brazil*. 2157.

6. Andrew Douglas. "What Animals Live in the Amazon Rainforest?" *World Atlas*, 20 Apr. 2022, worldatlas.com. Accessed 7 July 2022.

7. "Climate of Brazil." *Encyclopedia Britannica*, n.d., britannica.com. Accessed 7 July 2022.

8. Leildo M. Carilo Filho et al. "Natural History Predicts Patterns of Thermal Vulnerability in Amphibians from the Atlantic Rainforest of Brazil." *Ecology and Evolution*, 19 Nov. 2021, onlinelibrary.wiley.com. Accessed 7 July 2022.

9. "IBGE Launches Unprecedented Map of Biomes and Coastal-Marine System." *Agência IBGE Notícias*, 30 Oct. 2019, agenciadenoticias.ibge.gov.br. Accessed 4 Aug. 2022.

10. Jan Schipper. "Uruguayan Savanna." *One Earth*, 2022, oneearth.org. Accessed 7 July 2022.

11. Ana Cristina Campos. "Brazil Has 3,299 Animal and Plant Species under Threat." *Agência Brasil*, 5 Nov. 2020, agenciabrasil.ebc.com.br. Accessed 7 July 2022.

12. "Coral Snake." *Encyclopedia Britannica*, 2 May 2022, britannica.com. Accessed 7 July 2022.

13. Campos, "Brazil Has 3,299 Animal and Plant Species under Threat," *Agência Brasil*.

14. Balkovich et al., *Brazil*. 1697.

15. Balkovich et al., *Brazil*. 1681.

16. "Jaguar." *Encyclopedia Britannica*, 18 Feb. 2022, britannica.com. Accessed 7 July 2022.

CHAPTER 4. HISTORY

1. "The Brazilian Indians." *Survival*, 5 Mar. 2019, survivalinternational.org. Accessed 13 July 2022.

2. E. Bradford Burns et al. "Brazil." *Encyclopedia Britannica*, n.d., britannica.com. Accessed 7 July 2022.

3. Erik Ortiz. "What Is a Favela? Five Things to Know about Rio's So-Called Shantytowns." *NBC News*, 4 Aug. 2016, nbcnews.com. Accessed 7 July 2022.

4. Burns et al., "Brazil," *Encyclopedia Britannica*.

5. Burns et al., "Brazil," *Encyclopedia Britannica*.

6. "Brazil." *CIA World Factbook*, 1 July 2022, cia.gov. Accessed 7 July 2022.

CHAPTER 5. PEOPLE AND CULTURE

1. "Country Comparisons – Population." *CIA World Factbook*, 2022, cia.gov. Accessed 7 July 2022.
2. "Brazil Life Expectancy 1950–2022." *Macrotrends*, 2022, macrotrends.net. Accessed 7 July 2022.
3. Benjamin Elisha Sawe. "Largest Ethnic Groups in Brazil." *World Atlas*, 25 Apr. 2017, worldatlas.com. Accessed 7 July 2022.
4. "Brazil." *CIA World Factbook*, 1 July 2022, cia.gov. Accessed 7 July 2022.
5. "Indigenous Peoples in Brazil." *International Work Group for Indigenous Affairs*, n.d., iwgia.org. Accessed 7 July 2022.
6. "Indigenous Peoples in Brazil," *International Work Group for Indigenous Affairs*.
7. "Brazil," *CIA World Factbook*.
8. "Paulo Coelho Creates a Guinness World Record for Being the Most Translated Living Author for His Book 'The Alchemist.'" *News 18*, 14 Oct. 2014, news18.com. Accessed 7 July 2022.

CHAPTER 6. POLITICS

1. "Common Questions." *Government of Brazil*, 20 Jan. 2021, gov.br. Accessed 7 July 2022.
2. "Brazil," *CIA World Factbook*, 1 July 2022, cia.gov. Accessed 7 July 2022.
3. "Brazil," *CIA World Factbook*.
4. "Brazil." *Freedom House*, 2022, freedomhouse.org. Accessed 7 July 2022.
5. "The Legislature of Brazil," *Encyclopedia Britannica*, n.d., britannica.com. Accessed 7 July 2022.
6. "Brazil," *CIA World Factbook*.
7. Nelza Oliveira. "Brazilian Navy Celebrates 40 Years of Women Integration in the Force." *Diálogo Americas*, 24 Apr. 2020, dialogo-americas.com. Accessed 7 July 2022.

CHAPTER 7. ECONOMICS

1. "GDP (Current US$) – Brazil." *World Bank*, 2022, data.worldbank.org. Accessed 7 July 2022.

2. "Brazil." *CIA World Factbook*, 1 July 2022, cia.gov. Accessed 7 July 2022.

3. "The Brazilian Government Estimates R$ 700 Million in Investments to Develop the Fishing Industry." *Government of Brazil*, 15 Feb. 2022, gov.br. Accessed 7 July 2022.

4. "Hydropower Made Up 66% of Brazil's Electricity Generation in 2020." *US Energy Information Administration*, 7 Sept. 2021, eia.gov. Accessed 7 July 2022.

5. Sean Ross. "4 Countries That Produce the Most Food." *Investopedia*, 19 May 2022, investopedia.com. Accessed 7 July 2022.

6. Naomi Larsson. "The Million Dollar Cow: High-End Farming in Brazil – Photo Essay." *Guardian*, 10 May 2018, theguardian.com. Accessed 7 July 2022.

7. "Poultry." *Brazilian Farmers*, 2022, brazilianfarmers.com. Accessed 15 July 2022.

8. E. Bradford Burns et al. "Brazil." *Encyclopedia Britannica*, n.d., britannica.com. Accessed 7 July 2022.

9. Burns et al., "Brazil," *Encyclopedia Britannica*.

10. Burns et al., "Brazil," *Encyclopedia Britannica*.

11. Burns et al., "Brazil," *Encyclopedia Britannica*.

12. Claudio Paschoa. "There's Room to Grow on Brazil's Inland Waterways." *Marine Link*, 5 Jan. 2021, marinelink.com. Accessed 7 July 2022.

CHAPTER 8. BRAZIL TODAY

1. "Labor Force, Female (% of Total Labor Force) – Brazil." *World Bank*, 8 Feb. 2022, data.worldbank.org. Accessed 7 July 2022.

2. Paulo Cabral. "Indigenous Brazilians Educate Children in Their Native Language." *CGTN America*, 29 Mar. 2018, america.cgtn.com. Accessed 7 July 2022.

3. Carlos Monroy. "Education in Brazil." *World Education News & Reviews*, 14 Nov. 2019, wenr.wes.org. Accessed 7 July 2022.

4. Monroy, "Education in Brazil," *World Education News & Reviews*.

5. "Getting to Know Flamengo: Brazil's Most Popular Club." *FC Business*, 2022, fcbusiness.co.uk. Accessed 7 July 2022.

6. Manuela Andreoni. "Coronavirus in Brazil: What You Need to Know." *New York Times*, 19 Oct. 2021, nytimes.com. Accessed 4 Aug. 2022.

7. "Brazil Situation." *World Health Organization*, 7 July 2022, covid19.who.int. Accessed 7 July 2022.

8. "Brazil." *CIA World Factbook*, 1 July 2022, cia.gov. Accessed 7 July 2022.

ABOUT THE AUTHOR

ANDREA PELLESCHI

Andrea Pelleschi has worked as an editor in the education market for more than 20 years. She has a master of fine arts in creative writing from Emerson College and has written many nonfiction books for children and young adults.